# LIVING LIFE ON PURPOSE

Kenyetta Thigpen, PhD

BALBOA.
PRESS

A DIVISION OF HAY HOUSE

Balboa Press books may be ordered through booksellers or by contacting:

Balboa Press
A Division of Hay House
1663 Liberty Drive
Bloomington, IN 47403
www.balboapress.com
1 (877) 407-4847

Because of the dynamic nature of the Internet, any web addresses or links contained in this book may have changed since publication and may no longer be valid. The views expressed in this work are solely those of the author and do not necessarily reflect the views of the publisher, and the publisher hereby disclaims any responsibility for them.

The author of this book does not dispense medical advice or prescribe the use of any technique as a form of treatment for physical, emotional, or medical problems without the advice of a physician, either directly or indirectly. The intent of the author is only to offer information of a general nature to help you in your quest for emotional and spiritual well-being. In the event you use any of the information in this book for yourself, which is your constitutional right, the author and the publisher assume no responsibility for your actions.

Any people depicted in stock imagery provided by Getty Images are models, and such images are being used for illustrative purposes only. Certain stock imagery © Getty Images.

Print information available on the last page.

ISBN: 978-1-9822-2903-0 (sc)
ISBN: 978-1-9822-2904-7 (e)

Balboa Press rev. date:  06/21/2019

# TABLE OF CONTENTS

# DEDICATION

For Delores Ann Jeffrey and Ethel Glover

# CHAPTER 1

# Know Who You Are

For some of us as human beings we are born, we live, we die and in between, life kind of just happens. When we are young, we have parents or guardians who instruct us on the ways of life; learning from communities about the do's and the what not to do; and what is socially acceptable. In some societies, elders are respected and turned to for wisdom and guidance. Almost certainly there are rules and laws that are to be abided by as well as models to follow. Depending on the society, boys and girls grow up and marry to create tiny humans thus repeating the cycle of creation. Essentially, life as we know it is the same for just about all of us. How boring is that?

Many of us feel like we don't have a choice in the way our lives go. We feel trapped in many ways. We feel like life has no meaning creating a void that never seems to be fulfilled. Trying to fill that void leads us to constantly searching for meaning, asking the age-old question of "Why am I here?" or "What is my purpose?" We are great at creating the physical part of life. After all, having sex is quite fun and can be a pleasurable experience. We even follow rules well (well sort of, if overcrowding jails are any indication). We have been taught how to do everything except create the life we want- on purpose. Asking is only part of the equation; discovering helps us to put the pieces together and experience the comedy or tragedy of life. I want to impress upon you the notion that life doesn't just have to happen to us. William Ernest Henley wrote:

> "It matters not how straight the gate, how charged with punishments the scroll, I am the master of my fate, I am the captain of my soul"

This statement reigns true. We are the masters of our fate and we are certainly the captains of our souls. The issue is that we have been tragically misinformed about who, what, when, where, and how in just about everything. That's okay because discovery is part of the process. At some point, you will feel dissatisfied with a status quo life; you will think to yourself "there's got to be more to life than this". At some point you will question your belief systems. Systems that have been ingrained in you since birth. Questioning, becoming disgruntled and even angry is all part of the journey, so don't fret when you experience those feelings. These feelings are completely normal and will cause you to dig a little deeper for your higher purpose or calling, which ever you feel applies to you. There is more to life than just working, paying bills, and kicking the bucket. Life was meant to be lived and lived fully. You were meant to create the life that you want. You were meant to experience life on your terms and not let life just happen. You, dear soul was meant to create all aspects of your life, not just be a mere participant letting life knock you around at will. It wasn't that long ago that I too, questioned life. I must admit that I was very fearful. I lay awake many nights wondering what my future held. These questions and fears caused me to call out and go hunting if you will. I was hunting for truth, perspective, love, abundance that society said I couldn't have. I was hunting for so many things; truthfully, I still am hunting as I should be. Once you figure out what's been going on all these years when you felt like something was missing, you'll see that you were seeking answers and fulfillment for your life.

Our inner man is constantly reaching out to us, but we have been so programmed to not listen to it. We listen to literally everything else but what is on the inside of us. We listen to television, radio, social media, and well-meaning friends more than we listen to what our inner man is straining to tell us. I encourage you to practice listening to how you feel. If something in your "gut" is telling you to take a left, take the left. There is probably no traffic on the route or a parking space right by your work building when you get there. Learning how to flow with your feelings will serve you immensely on your journey to abundance, love, enlightenment or whatever your desires for your life are. There are so many things your soul can help you with. If you want to be guided to the career or job that fulfills you, done. If you want to be led to the best produce at the supermarket, done. If you want the best deals on a new suit, done. Sounds like magic. Maybe, but my point is, whatever your desires are start on the inside of you, not on the outside. Everything you need is already there, waiting for you to gain the knowledge to access it. Know that whatever you need, your spirit/soul/inner man will guide you to it!

By now you are probably thinking "alright, I know I have a soul, I know it's supposed to help me, got it, how is that going to help me create life or manifest my desires?" While manifesting is the proof of the pudding, the journey on the way to the manifestation is the juicy part. Recognizing you have power and learning how to use that power is truly liberating. One of the things you have to realize is you are more powerful than you think. This power is housed at the tip of your tongue. A question to ask yourself is what are you saying about yourself, about your life? Do you believe you deserve a good life? What would a good life look like to you? Would it be a great job, beautiful wife, 3.5 kids, and a house with a white picket fence? Or would it be helping to plant trees in a remote village, or running a homeless shelter? Basically, the "good life" looks different for everyone. There is no right or wrong way to live your life because it's your life; you do whatever you want with it. Understand that you have the power to create the life you want whether it's good or bad. Let's go back to the question of what are you saying about yourself? Do you think you are worthy of a good life? This is a major starting point because we are told we are unworthy. We are just mere human beings, surely, we don't deserve good health, money, and beach vacations. Surely, we must struggle through life, right? I'm going to go with no! Struggling doesn't feel good and I'm going to go out on a limb here and say there has got to be a better way to do life. Lo and behold, there is. First, you have to know you are worthy of all the good the universe can give you. You were meant to be right here, right now, and your sweet soul deserves it. You just do. I want you to stop right now and say, "I AM WORTHY!" Say it out loud and when you do, I want you to feel it in your bones, feel it in your soul. Let your worthiness resonate within you.

If you don't feel you are worthy of the life you deserve, you won't ask for it; let alone have it. So, let's start there, you are worthy of the life of your choice. No matter what you have done in the past, no matter your religious beliefs, sexual orientation, the color of your skin, your choice to eat chicken, beef, or pork; you are worthy. Once you understand you are worthy, you can halt the negative talks that you have with yourself in your head. You can challenge the beliefs which no longer serve you and put into place things that help you to maneuver through life. Let me take a moment to say how proud I am of you right now. I am proud you picked up this book and I am immensely proud you kept on reading. Even if you stop right now, I am still proud of your growth thus far. You are probably thinking to yourself, "So, I have a soul/inner man; I listen to it, and I'm worthy, now what?" I am so grateful you asked.

# CHAPTER 2

# You Are More Powerful Than You Think

Most people go through their lives letting life happen to them. They create life by default, not fully understanding their creative power. For example, a person might say something like "I'm never going to get a better job", or "I never have any money", you know, those type of negative things. I guarantee the person who says those things, probably experiences lack of abundance in their life and has a job they hate. Do you know people who say, "If it isn't one thing it's another?", or "when it rains it pours?" I know people who talk like this all of the time. They may be moms, dads, grandparents, aunts, uncles, co-workers, and best friends. Whether we realize it or not, we are constantly creating, either on purpose or by default. One concept many people have not grasped is understanding everything is energy.

Everything has a vibration and is in constant motion even if you don't see it moving. The chair you are sitting in has a vibration to it; albeit a low one, but a vibration, nonetheless. This book you are holding has an energy signature. Animals and people consist of, you guessed it energy. Now, I want to let you in on a little secret you can share; words have vibrations too. Think about this for a minute. Words have the ability to instantly change the way you feel. If someone says something negative to you, you probably feel bad or sad. However, if someone tells you how beautiful or handsome you look, you put a little extra pep in your step. Some researchers have conducted studies in which positive things were spoken to plants versus negative things. The plants received the positive messages flourished while the negative control group did not grow as well. Can you imagine what would happen to us if we focused on the positive aspects around us? Your words really do have power and it is liberating to harness power to create your life on purpose and not by default. Maybe you are not experiencing your life the way you think you should. Maybe you want more out of life than what you are currently getting.

I want to encourage you to change what you are saying to yourself, about yourself, and about your life in general. Start speaking, well, life! I know it may be easier said than done, with all the distractions around you. So much of what is on television is not positive. Basically, we have to work really hard to not be discouraged with what is on the daily news or pick any social media platform and there is bound to be something that will upset you within minutes. While, I can't tell you what to do, I would encourage you to limit your time with those media outlets. I understand it is important we remain informed, but I wouldn't eat, breathe, and sleep the daily news around the clock either. Try programs which nourish your inner man. My friends will say to me "Hey, did you see...? (insert literally any program); then they say "Oh, I forgot, you don't watch television". Too much of it is negative and stifling and makes me feel sad. I bet I am not the only one who feels like this. Try for one week limiting your social media and television use and see what happens. I guarantee you are going to feel better. Maybe go for a walk instead, get the blood pumping in those limbs. I know after a long day's work, you don't want to do much other than eat, take a shower, watch television and go to bed. If you have a family, those things probably don't get done in that order, and you rarely have time for yourself, let alone go for a walk. But there is something about being outside, breathing fresh air and listening to the birds chirping. You will feel a sense of peace that will resonate with you that you won't get sitting on your sofa.

To create your life on purpose you have to do things differently. If the practices you currently have in place have not led you to a place of bliss, then maybe you could try something different, like reading this book. I mean, doing something different can't hurt. If none of what you are reading moves you; then you can always go back to what you have always been doing and your life will be the same. However, I believe if you shift your thinking just a little bit, you will notice a change. If you just decide to be open to the wonders the universe will place literally at your feet, you will never be the same, and neither will the people around you. They will wonder why you are so happy all of the time while everything around you seems to be in chaos. Chaos might be a strong word, but some places of employment can feel like navigating a battlefield at times trying not to end up behind enemy lines.

We've already talked about knowing who you are and the power you have to speak over your life. Understanding you are part of the energy that creates worlds is a powerful notion. You, my dear sweet soul have creative energy vibrating back and forth on the inside of you. The trick is to line up with the source energy on the inside of you. Everything around you started with a thought, then there were words, and then there was action. Every plane, house, book, dish, movie, dance, gym, restaurant, everything began with a thought. What we want to do is pay attention to our thoughts because those thoughts become reality in our lives. Now, this is not to say you must monitor every thought you have, that could be a daunting task at best. Then, you would be nervous about all the less than stellar thoughts you might be having. The goal is to recognize the feelings you have. If a thought makes you feel uneasy, shift those thoughts into something positive or something that makes you feel better. Thoughts that make you feel joyous and happy; those are the thoughts you want to focus on. You have the power to create worlds at your disposal so why not use it to your advantage. Create the life you desire on purpose by understanding your power comes from within and not an outside source. Know that your inner man will guide you and instruct you in creating life on purpose. The trick is to strengthen your inner man muscle.

# CHAPTER 3

# Strengthening Your Inner Man

S trengthening your inner man is just like working out and lifting weights. Picture a person with a lean but maybe small physique at your local gym. You see this person come to the gym for the first time and they are timid, they don't know how to use the machines and they seem awkward. They get a trainer and the trainer shows them how to use the equipment that would best serve them and puts them on a plan to increase their strength. That person starts to lift weights, beginning with the ten-pound weights first. A month or so passes by and you notice subtle changes in that person's physique. You also notice they seem a little bit more confident just by the way they walk around in the gym. They are arm curling twenty-five-pound dumbbells. Now, they look people in the eye when they speak to others, they even ask to work in some reps on a machine you are using. You are quite surprised because you remember when they first came and how unsure they were. Now, they seem confident.

Well, building your inner man is a similar process. Strengthening your inner man is not something achieved right away. The inner man has been neglected for so long, the process must begin slowly and gradually increase. You wouldn't go to the gym and attempt to bench press 300 pounds your first time there. Well, you could but you could seriously injure yourself and delay your progress. Plus, you would be discouraged thinking "I just can't do it!" Strengthening your inner man requires you do put in the work, just like you would at the gym. You must do things to work inner man muscle. In your mind you may be thinking, "Work out inner man, got it, how do I do that?" There is no one way to strengthen your inner man muscle, but you can start with things to feed your inner man/soul. For example, these days plenty of people meditate. Meditation is a practice in which people essentially still their mind. There have to be over a hundred ways to meditate but most people associate meditation with sitting in a quiet room, on a mat, legs crossed, and chanting, or humming, or whatever clears your mind. If that type of meditation practice resonates with you, then by all means, do it! Now, if you are like me and pressed for time, you might not have the time to sit in a quiet room, on a mat, legs crossed, and chanting. I mean, if you have kids, it's probably NOT going to happen. It's like their little spirits are tuned to when you wake up. What I found that works for me is listening to meditation songs on the way to work in my car. Of course, I can't close my eyes and chant because, well, I'm driving, and that could be bad, really bad. These songs put me in a calm state which helps me throughout my day.

Another way to help strengthen your inner man is to listen to or read books you feel led to. I like to read versus listening to books simply because I take notes and like to highlight my books. Electronic version books have the same capability but I'm a little old school and like to turn the pages with my fingers. However, many people enjoy listening to books because it allows them to move around and do things versus sitting and reading. There are literally thousands of books to choose from but choose the ones that seem to move you. Look at the titles, say them aloud, ask your spirit "What do you think?" and if the books seem to call to you, then go for it. I encourage you to remain open to everything the universe sends your way. You might be at the local bookstore looking at a book and a nice lady notices you reading the back of said book. She interjects, "Oh, my goodness! I read that book, totally changed my life!" So then, you think "Ok, maybe I'll check it out". Then she says, "Hey listen, here's my email, when you finish reading the book we can get together and maybe have a book review or something." And just like that, a friendship begins. The universe will bring people to you to help you along your journey. I am always picking up books I find interesting, but I noticed in the past I might not have been ready for them. When that happens, I just put them to the side until I feel called to them again. Knowledge is awesome but you don't want too much of it all at once, it can be overwhelming. When you go to a buffet restaurant no matter how yummy everything looks, you simply cannot eat everything there.

I have also found workshops are helpful to help strengthen the inner man. Once again, the universe will lead you to the resources that you need. Some years ago, a wonderful lady was conducting a class in the city I lived in. At the time I hadn't heard anything about universal laws, but it seemed interesting, so I signed up and went to the class, and I was the only one there. During the workshop we talked about deliberate intention and vision boards. Here again, I had never heard of this stuff so needless to say, I was very skeptical. I put my picture in the middle of the canvas board and told her I would put the rest on later. I didn't actually complete the vision board, but I ordered the book she taught the class from. I didn't read the book until five years later. What I didn't know was one workshop set me on a path which totally changed my life. One workshop led me to read one book, and another, and another. The coolest thing about the universe is there will be opportunities for you to share with others. I was able to share this information with a very dear friend. As a result, they have achieved everything on their vision board and looking to add more. It is so much fun to see the light bulb come on and see when people create their life on purpose.

Workshops you feel called to are great, because you get the opportunity to interact with people who have the same interest as you. Many times, you might share something someone really needed, and those times can be times of great healing. Strengthening your inner man will allow you to be more in tune with what the universe is trying to say to you. The laws governing the universe will be made clear to you and you can have a much clearer picture of how you want your life to proceed.

# CHAPTER 4

# Universal Laws

It is important to understand universal laws exist. These laws don't discriminate or pick and choose who they work for. Essentially, they work much like gravity. We know what goes up must come down, unless there is some type of apparatus holding it up. The laws of the universe work for everyone whether they are aware of them or not. For example, let's say you get up in the morning and stump your toe on the way to the bathroom, then you get shampoo in your eye, and you can't find your keys. You say to yourself, not even out loud, "Geez, can this day get any worse?" You hop into your car; already late mind you, and get on the expressway and to your dismay, there is a traffic jam and you will be late for your work meeting that which starts at 8:00 a.m. So, you see, your day really did get worse.

In a nutshell, you attract what you think about. Earlier, we mentioned thoughts eventually turn into reality. The good thing is realities can be changed because, you guessed it; thoughts can be changed. The universe gives you what you ask for even if those things are less desired events. How many people do you know are always thinking doom and gloom? Every time you call them on the phone, something is always wrong. They might even say "things are just awful, I never have any money but I'm okay, I guess". I am pretty sure these particular people always have something going on. There is always some kind of drama or problem. You, trying to be a good friend, daughter, or whatever role you have in their lives, want to be sympathetic to whatever it is vexing them at the time. So, you console them time after time about their situation, and sure enough, the same thing or some variation of is happening to you! You get the same ailment, your car breaks down, your bank account goes into overdraft, and to top it all off, you have an issue with a coworker. There is a very old saying "birds of a feather flock together". The more attention you pay to these types of issues; the more in tune to their frequencies you become. This is not to say ignore your friends, but you can try to speak positive things to them instead of buying a ticket on their pity train. This way, you are still being supportive but not opening yourself up to unwanted desires. Focusing on unwanted things creates the very thing you do not want.

We must realize nothing just shows up out of the blue into our experience. At some point, we attracted it to us, whether wanted or unwanted. Think of yourself as a powerful magnet, like the big ones you might see in an action movie. You, the magnet picks up thoughts along the way as you are constantly thinking, unless you are asleep, then all attraction stops. Anyway, you pick up one thought, then another, then another, and soon, your magnet is overflowing with all these thoughts which may or may not serve you. What you think about, you will get more of. The universe gives you more of what you pay attention to. A little over a year ago, I was practicing bringing things into my awareness. At the time I would focus on a Mercedes Benz car and say, "I can afford that". I started to see more Mercedes Benz cars every day on my way to work and on the way home. I decided I would count all the Mercedes Benz cars just to see how many would show up into my awareness, since, you know, I was focusing my attention and all. One day I counted over 300 Mercedes Benz cars, in one day!!! I was amazed! Fast forward another year, I decided I would focus on one Mercedes. It was a Mercedes GLC Coupe which I thought was nice. I started focusing on one and started seeing up to 5 to 8 of those trucks a day. Now, I live in a city where folks driving Mercedes is common and these cars were probably always on the roads, but they were not brought into my awareness until I focused on them. What you pay attention to, is what the universe will give you. Understanding universal laws will cause you to take notice of what you are paying attention to. In other words, you will be more cognizant of what you are thinking about. Once you see the effect your thoughts have on your life, I just know you will be willing to shift your thinking because you will want to live life-on purpose. The universe will give you what you ask for even if it is a less than desired event because the universe gives you the freedom to choose. It's not going to say, "Hold on now, are you sure you want that?" You have all the power and can utilize that power however you see fit. It's your life. Do you want to live life on purpose or by default? The universe is going to support you, either way. Giving thought to something is just like dropping it right into your lap.

Another universal law at work is deliberate creation. There are two parts to this law; one is the thought of what you want and the other is the expectation, belief, or allowing of what you are creating through the thought that you are thinking. Let's say you have been thinking about a new job. You have done the research, filled out the application, and updated your resume. You have even gone so far as to look for places to live in the new city where your new job will be. It goes without saying that you are excited about this new opportunity. This law goes right to work creating whatever it is you are thinking about. At this point, you are allowing what you are wanting to come into your experience and no doubt the new job opportunity is on its way. Then, in your excitement you tell a friend about the new job opportunity, the city you will move to, you even tell them what you plan to do with the increased pay, and all of the cool places you plan to visit. Your excitement is uncontainable. And then, they say "So, what are the requirements for the job? Do you think you are qualified for the job? I mean there's got to be like what 100 people applying for the same job. I mean I'm not trying to be negative; I'm just being realistic; I don't want your feelings to be hurt if you don't get it?" Suddenly, your excitement tanks. You feel as if a cold bucket of water has been thrown on you. Your stomach coils and then you start to wonder if you are qualified for the job. Your mind continues to wonder about the other 100 or more applicants and if they might be more qualified than you. Now, at this point, you are not allowing what you want to come into your experience, your flow has stopped. Think of your life as being a stream, constantly flowing. Sometimes your stream moves fast, sometimes at a slower pace. Nevertheless, the stream is always moving. When you have negative thoughts or negative emotion about something or an experience you want; you throw resistance like an old tire into your stream and so what you want, like the new job halts its movement to you. It is being blocked by that old tire (negative thought). Now, don't think you will never have a negative thought ever in your life because that just wouldn't be life. Life gives you contrast or situations and experiences that cause you to ask for something. This is part of your creative power. For example, the lack of money causes you to ask or desire more money into your experience.

The universe immediately gets to work on bringing you money. It is not your job to figure out how you will get the money you desire. The universe will drop into your spirit ideas bringing you the abundance you want such as a new business idea. However, if you say, "I'm never going to get any money", or "I'm always going to be broke", you stop your abundance in its tracks. The abundance you want is chugging along as the grant for your small business loan is being worked out. A reputable business partner who has more capital has even agreed to come on board because they believe in your vision for your company. Then, a debt letter comes in the mail and you say "Gosh, I am never going to get ahead, I just don't see how some people make it and I can't seem to get a break! It's not fair!" Screech!!! That is the sound of your abundance making its way to you slamming on the brakes. Understand there will be times when you feel discouraged and you will experience fear and doubt. However, the goal is to recognize those feelings, fears, and doubts and turn toward a better feeling thought. Those doubts, fears, and negative emotions knock you out of alignment with your source/ inner guidance system you have on the inside of you. Think of your inner guidance system as a GPS of sorts. We all have one either on our phone and most newer vehicles have some sort of navigation system. That sick feeling you get when you are experiencing a negative emotion or thought is your inner guidance system saying, "Whoa there, that thought does not serve you". That's your cue to say" Wait a minute! The universe always has my back and I know that this situation is going to work out, no matter what!" You will be surprised at what a simple shift in thinking will do for whatever it is you are going through.

Another piece of living life on purpose is the practice of allowing. Allowing is the practice of allowing things in your life to unfold in a way that still allows you to be connected to your inner being. I know that I used allowed three times in the same sentence, but this concept is important. Many times, we as human beings want to sway people over to our way of thinking, because it is so much better than theirs (insert sarcasm). Doing this can undoubtedly cause you much grief and despair because no one wants to be told what to do, even toddlers. You and I both know if you tell a small child not to touch something, they are most certainly going to touch that thing you told them not to touch, probably several times, right in your face! While you may desire for your friends, family, and partners to experience the joy and bliss that you do, you must know you cannot create for another person and allowing them to have their own creative experiences is most beneficial. True, you will not always agree with others about certain issues and that is fine. However, allow them the space to grow and have their own experiences just as you have yours.

One thing to think about is the difference between tolerating and allowing. Tolerating has a negative emotion attached to it, while allowing doesn't. If you say to yourself, "You know what? I'm just going to let people do whatever they want and be whoever they want to be, even if I don't like it". At this moment, you feel negative emotion which isn't allowing. Allowing does not have a negative emotion riding on its coattails which therein lies your freedom. Allowing puts you in a place where you no longer attract unwanted experiences because you purposely choose not to make them part of your reality. This is powerful because you always have a choice in how you want your life to unfold. Once you decide to recognize how you are thinking about your life, you can avoid many of the pitfalls that dump resistance in your stream. Going through life having wonderful experiences is like swimming in your very own backyard stream of life.

We can probably agree swimming downstream is a whole lot easier than swimming upstream, against the current. Resistance causes you to swim upstream which can be both physically and mentally exhausting. Salmon and a few other species of fish swim upstream for the purpose of laying their eggs. However, we are not fish. (We are human beings who have consciousness that allows us to live a life of our choosing). How exciting is it to know you have a choice? Life just doesn't just have to happen. It doesn't have to be "that's just the way life is."

There is freedom and power in creating the life you want on purpose. All of the tools you need are already on the inside of you, you just need the access code to download all of the programs to benefit you in creating the life you desire. By digging deeper and tuning into your inner guidance system you will be able to fine tune your frequency to receive what you are asking for in your life.

# CHAPTER 5

# Getting From Here to There

By now you are probably racking your brain trying to figure out how you are going to get all of this to work. It is working right now. The universe is guiding you to the resources you need in order to live your life on purpose. Try not to think about the laws working for others and not you although I totally understand your frustration at this point. You might think you will have to constantly monitor your thoughts and you must stop yourself from thinking "bad" thoughts. Negative emotions are going to come, it is your inner guidance system directing you to a better feeling thought or emotion. A good rule of thumb is to pay attention to how you feel about, well, everything. A lot of people say, "listen to your gut". This is true in many instances. If you have a bad feeling about a business deal, then you probably want to steer clear of the deal. If you go to buy a car and "something" is telling you to wait, you probably want to wait. The universe will help you in getting you what you want.

Years ago, I purchased a 2007 Honda Accord. My Nissan Sentra had literally burned up in my driveway, so I kind of needed a new car. I was looking for a Honda dealership but couldn't find it and I had decided to turn around and go back home (I was visiting my parents at the time). When I turned around, I saw a billboard directing me to the dealership I was looking for. I went into the dealership and told them about the ad I saw online. They did not have the car I was looking for and yes, I was heartbroken because I really needed a car that I could afford. The universe was still working it out, and at the time I knew nothing about universal laws, an inner guidance system, or anything of that nature. The salesman agreed to sell me the Honda Accord they had available for the price that was in the ad! Whoa!!! look at the universe work. I was able to purchase the car with no money down and I didn't need a co-signer.

You can imagine my elation. Purchasing a car in my own name was a big deal at the time. Did I mention I didn't have a job? No, I didn't have a job as I had moved to a new city. However, I had enough money from the insurance company that totaled my car to pay the car note and insurance on the car for six months! So, you see, the universe is always working it out for you, always. Now, suppose I had hopped onto the interstate instead of listening to that "something" and gone another way? If I had done that, I would have missed the huge billboard showing me where the dealership was and possibly missed out on a great opportunity to buy a new car.

Listening to your inner man is important and the more you practice using it, the more in tune you will be. I practice on the way to a crowded shopping area thinking about a parking space. When I get there, there are either many parking spaces available or there is just one spot left, just for me! When I get a parking spot, I am grateful for that spot because I know there are more available parking spots coming for another day. Now how cool is that? Yes, it's just a simple parking spot but just imagine saying what you want, and that thing or experience comes your way almost immediately?

As mentioned before, once you decide, the universe gets to work right away to give you what you asked for. Therefore, it is important to understand that thoughts become things and things become a part of your reality. Getting a hold of this concept will put you well on your way to creating the life you want on purpose and not by default. No longer will life be beating you about. If something does come into your experience that you do not want, you can shift your thoughts and feelings and change that part of your reality.

Struggling to get the universal laws to work for you will cause more resistance to be in your way because you are thinking about it from an action standpoint. Think about your journey from a vibration or frequency standpoint. If on the way to work you listen to a program on 104.6 FM, you wouldn't turn your channel to 1190 AM, would you? If you did, you would miss the program. The universal laws work much the same way. Life causes you to ask and the universe goes immediately to work getting what you desire to you. However, if you are not a vibrational match to what you asked for, it's not going to come until you are a vibrational match to it.

Money is probably the one thing we all have a need for because well let's face it, money allows us to eat, play, and get the most basic things we need. We all need a place to live, food to eat, and clothes to put on. Sometimes we want or need more abundance in order to do the things we want to do in life. You may want to buy a newer car, or a house, or just take a vacation. Working from paycheck to paycheck is not your ideal existence.

I do not blame you. So, life causes us to ask for more money. Immediately things start moving in your favor. You don't see things working, but they are working. Now what you have to do is line up with abundance on its way. In order to do that, you must think of things not as they are but as you want them to be. Think like the abundance is already there. Granted, that bill that just came in the mail is really there sitting on the dining room table. You see it, your wife sees it, you see it every time you pass by on the way to the kitchen. The bill is there but the money is not. Well, it's not there yet. However, you don't want to stop it by saying things like "I don't know how I'm going to get more money" or "If it's not one thing it's another".

I know this is easier said than done but when you notice yourself going down a negative emotion road, pull to the side and say to yourself "I know the universe is working it out for me, all of the time." Sometimes we focus so much on what we don't have that it keeps us in a vibrational holding pattern matching us to what we don't want. Have you ever been traveling on an airplane and your flight has to wait for a runway to land? The pilot might circle the airport in a flight pattern until they are cleared to land. The same concept can be applied to lining up with what you want. Holding yourself in a vibrational holding pattern to what you don't want only puts the brakes on what you have asked for.

As mentioned earlier, everything around us has a vibration or frequency. In fact, we human beings are vibrational beings. We are emitting signals too like a large radio tower. Our words and thoughts go out and attract back to us through the signals we send out. It is a good idea to say great, happy, and abundant things so we can attract those things back to us. If we don't want doom and gloom in our life, then let's not think doom and gloom in our life. I want you to think back to the person you know is always talking about how sick they are and how much money they don't have and how nothing good ever happens to them. Just take a moment and really think about all the conversations you have had with this person. Think about all the times you have visited with them and what they were saying. It was mostly negative right? I recommend you speak positive things into your life, you will thank yourself for it. Speaking positive things will align you to your inner source. Your source is always directing you to the good in life. When you say negative things about yourself or other situations, you feel bad, anxious, or even depressed. These emotions indicate that you are not in alignment with your source. Your source is not going to agree with the negative things you are thinking or saying which is why those emotions are designed to have you redirect your thoughts. What an awesome guidance system.

## Fine Tuning

Fine tuning your vibrational frequency will certainly help you to manifest the life that you are asking for. One way to fine tune your frequency is to practice daily. I find setting the intention for my day helps to get my day going in the way that I desire. Everyone wants to have a good day I presume so it's a good idea start as soon as you wake up; before checking emails or getting on social media. It is very rare any internet news will give you a warm and fuzzy feeling, in fact most news does the opposite. At any rate; setting the intention for the day when you wake up is essential to getting positive momentum flowing. I start by being grateful for the new day and the opportunity to create great things. Once I am out of the bed, I pull out my journal. I have found journaling is a great way to not only envision my life as I want it to be; but I can go back and take a look at all of the things manifested I wrote in my journal and which is really exciting. An example of one of my journal entries is as follows:

November 21, 2017

"I am excited to be here this morning. This time is valuable, and I look forward to manifesting the desired results in my life. I see myself as a total package and I know that I am enough! I AM ENOUGH, in fact, I am more than enough. In this picture of more than enough, I am excited, smiling, happy, and full of energy as I move about my day. I have fruitful conversations and I am attracting only those people who are in harmony with my current vibration. I am unlimited in all facets of my life. My bank account is unlimited. My decisions are not based on what I can afford but my desires because I am a magnet that attracts abundance to myself. I choose unlimited abundance because there is more than enough. I see myself surrounded by others who want growth. Today I will make a note of all the things that make me happy."

This journal entry was written roughly two years ago. Since then, I have changed many of the things I write down. Journaling shouldn't take more than ten minutes or so. In addition, a journal entry doesn't have to be very long. Sometimes I would write a page and some days maybe a few paragraphs. Just be led to write whatever comes to mind. Direct your life by setting the intention early and watch how your day flows. I really try to journal first thing in the morning before I start getting ready for the day. Sometimes I will take my journal with me with the intention of journaling when I get a break, which never happens. I try to journal even if it's only for a few minutes. Your journal entry can include whatever you desire to see unfold in your life. At the time that journal entry was written, I was struggling with some negative emotion concerning my self-esteem. I was working on knowing I was enough! Many times, our society convinces us we are not enough to accomplish our dreams. We are not enough to handle a more challenging task at work. We are too big or too small. We're too short or too tall. We're not enough for this guy or that girl. There are so many things the world tells us we are not. What you must realize is you my dear friend are more than enough for whatever it is you want to do with your life. Period!

Another practice I found helps to fine tune my frequency is listening to music that soothes or inspires my inner man. I have several playlists I use almost daily. My morning gratitude playlist includes songs about gratitude and thankfulness. The prosperity and abundance playlist include songs about prosperity, abundance, and mantras help direct intention. The meditation playlist songs are beneficial for meditating as well as centering thoughts and intention. Many people use music platforms for exercising, and it would be easy as a basic search for songs to help you along your journey. Some days after a difficult day at work, you might find listening to an abundance song will help melt the stress away. Or, when a bill comes in and you are noticing lack instead of abundance, listening to abundance songs are helpful. There are many ways to help you fine tune your frequency. However, choose what resonates with you. Some practices are not for everyone, which is okay. Some people enjoy Rock music while others might enjoy Jazz or Classical music. There is no one way to do anything, only what moves you on your journey.

Each person's journey is different and specific to them so while meditation in a room, on a mat, with a fountain trickling in the background might work for some people; that scenario might totally put you to sleep. Find a method or a combination of things that work for you.

Once you are well on your way to discovering your inner man and fine tuning your frequency to attract all that you desire; you will be tempted to isolate yourself or at least be with like-minded people such as yourself. You can still hang out with your friends and go to holiday dinners with your family. The goal is to be able to maneuver within your world and attract with your new way of thinking what you really want in your life and not attract by default. By living life on purpose, you will be able to have the life that you have created with your own thoughts. There is power in your creation. There is power in your thoughts. There is power on the inside of you waiting to burst forth and assist you with the creative process. Remember that you are a divine being and all that you do is powerful and creative in every way.

Printed in the United States
By Bookmasters